DISNEY MOANA
THE BEAT OF YOUR HEART
A Musical Exploration Activity Book

HAL•LEONARD®

Explore an interactive experience online!
Go to: **halleonard.com/exploremusic/00160410**

*The publisher gratefully acknowledges Tiana Nonasina Liufau
for her expertise and contribution to the creation of this book.*

Printed in the United States of America

ISBN 978-1-4950-6478-4

Published by Hal Leonard LLC
7777 W. Bluemound Road
P.O. Box 13819
Milwaukee, WI 53213

CONTENTS

THE BEAT
is All Around You

Moana lives on the beautiful, green island of Motunui. She is the daughter of the chief. She loves the ocean and the sound it makes when it crashes upon the shore, like the beating of the island drums.

Moana lives with her father Chief Tui, her mother Sina, her Gramma Tala, her rooster friend Heihei, and her pet pig Pua. She learned the stories and songs of her ancestors and feels their rhythms in her heart.

THE BEAT
is Inside You

Y ou can play the drum like Moana, but first you must feel the beat.

GET READY TO PLAY!

Show the beat with your whole body. Sit cross-legged on the floor and bounce your knees to a steady beat.

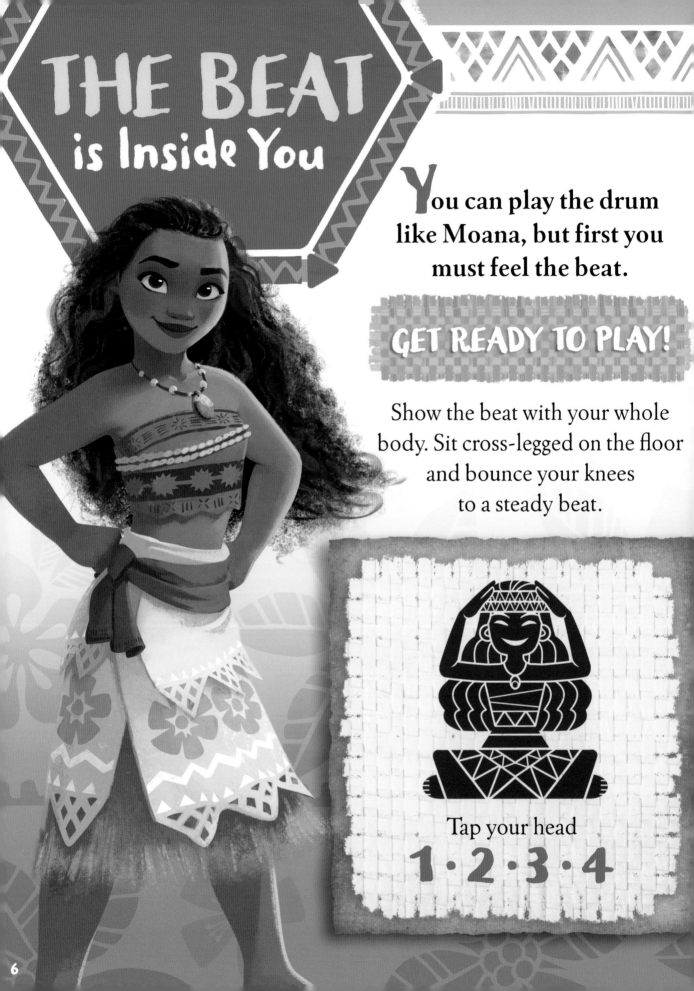

Tap your head
1 · 2 · 3 · 4

Cross your arms and
pat your shoulders

1 · 2 · 3 · 4

Tap your chest to
show the heartbeat

1 · 2 · 3 · 4

Tap your knees

1 · 2 · 3 · 4

Tap the floor
with both hands

1 · 2 · 3 · 4

SEE
MORE
ONLINE

THE BEAT
is in Your Clapping
PART 1

Show the beat in your clapping. **Pati** is clapping with your palms flat. **Po** is clapping with your palms cupped.

Clap **pati** four times, then clap **po** four times.

pati

po

GET READY TO PLAY!

1 · 2 · 3 · 4

1 · 2 · 3 · 4

SEE MORE ONLINE

9

THE BEAT
is in Your Clapping
PART 2

Make your clapping more exciting by adding other motions.

Pati high (by your forehead)

Po low (by your tummy)

Tap your knees

Tap the floor

GET READY TO PLAY!

Pati

1 · 2 · 3 · 4

Po

1 · 2 · 3 · 4

Tap your knees

1 · 2 · 3 · 4

Tap the floor

1 · 2 · 3 · 4

What other motions can you do?

SEE MORE ONLINE

Create Your Own MOTIONS

Imagine that you are traveling with Moana on her amazing ocean journey. Add motions to your clapping to help tell the story.

Sit cross-legged on the floor and bounce your knees up and down to the beat.

GET READY TO PLAY!

Shout out a word and do the motions.

FISH!

Move your hands like
a fish in the water

BIRD!

Move your arms like
a flying bird

SWIM!

Move like you
are swimming

ROW!

Move like you
are rowing a canoe

Can you think of other motions to do? Trade off your
motions with **pati** and **po** clapping patterns.

SEE
MORE
ONLINE

The LALI

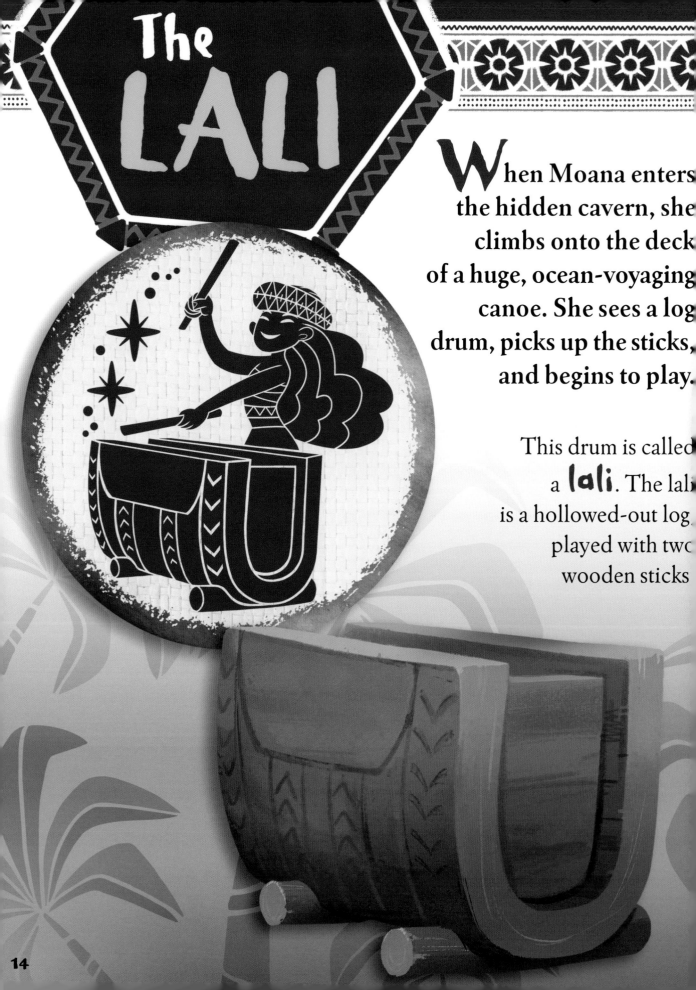

When **W**hen Moana enters the hidden cavern, she climbs onto the deck of a huge, ocean-voyaging canoe. She sees a log drum, picks up the sticks, and begins to play.

This drum is called a **lali**. The lali is a hollowed-out log, played with two wooden sticks

Lali drums are used to communicate over long distances. They can signal an important event like a ceremony, the end of a war, or the arrival of a chief from a neighboring village.

GET READY TO PLAY!

Practice the lali by tapping your knees two times and then the floor two times while chanting:

LA – LA   LI – LI

Make and Play a LALI

You can make and play a **lali** of your own.

You will need an empty box with an opening on the top and two wooden spoons. (Ask an adult to cut the opening on the box.)

Hold a spoon in each hand and play your **lali** by drumming the top of the box.

Play the drum twice. Use both spoons at the same time, close together in the center of the box.

LA — LA

Play the drum twice. Use both spoons at the same time, wide apart on the the box.

LI — LI

SEE MORE ONLINE

Make and Play a FALA

When Moana was a little girl, she sat with the other children on woven mats to hear the stories told by Gramma Tala.

These mats are called **fala**. They are woven from the leaves of the pandanus plant. The **fala** can be played like a drum when it is rolled tightly into a cylinder and tied with rope.

The **fala** is played with two sticks and is used to accompany singers and dancers.

Speak or sing this chant and pat your knees to the beat.

FA – LA   FA – LA

You can make your own **fala**.
Roll up a newspaper or woven
placemat and beat it
with sticks or spoons.

SEE
MORE
ONLINE

Make and Play a PAHU

When Moana is older, she will be a great leader of her people.

The **pahu** is the leader of the drum family. The pahu is carved from a single log of a coconut tree and covered on the playing end with stretched sharkskin. It is played with the palms and fingers of the hands.

Speak this chant and pat your knees to the beat of the **pahu**.

PA – HU   PA – HU

To make your own **pahu**, turn a plastic bucket over and drum it with your hands.

SEE MORE ONLINE

Make and Play a FA'ATETE

Moana and Maui work together to achieve their mission.

The **fa'atete** is like the pahu, but smaller and played with sticks. It has a higher sound and usually plays a faster pattern. The fa'atete and the pahu work together.

GET READY TO PLAY!

The **pahu** plays the steady beat and the **fa'atete** plays faster. Speak this chant and pat your knees to the rhythm twice as fast. You can play both hands together or switch hands left and right.

PA – HU PA – HU

FA'-A TE-TE FA'-A TE-TE

To make your own **fa'atete**, use a large oatmeal container with two pencils for drumsticks.

SEE MORE ONLINE

Create a DRUM Celebration

After Moana's successful journey, the plants and animals return to Motunui, and the island thrives once again. The villagers are overjoyed, and welcome Moana home.

Join the celebration with your drumming. Play the pattern below in different ways.

Beat

Beat

Fast - er

Beat

GET READY TO PLAY!

Pati

Po

Tap your knees

Tap the floor

SEE
MORE
ONLINE

Tell The Story of Your Own
JOURNEY

You can be a wayfinder like Moana. Create your own adventure and use drumming to tell your story.

PATI   PO

LA — LI

FA – LA

FA' – A

TE – TE

PA – HU

What Did You LEARN?

The **beat** is all around you—in your clapping, and even inside of you.

You can tell the story of your own journey through rhythm and movement.

You can make and play a **lali**.

You can make and play a **fala**.

You can make and play a **pahu**.

You can make
and play a
fa'atete.

THE BEAT of Your Heart

There's a rhythm in the falling rain.
There's a rhythm in our sweet land.
There's a rhythm in the bright blue ocean waves,
Playing music on the sand.

There's rhythm all around you,
And there's rhythm deep inside.
You can feel it pounding deep in your heart.
So just let your heart be your guide.

It's the beat, beat, beat of your heart.
Feel your heart beat right from the start.
And you can hum, hum, hum as you drum on a drum
With the beat, beat, beat of your heart.

It's the beat, beat, beat of your heart.
Feel your heart beat right from the start.
And you can hum, hum, hum as you drum on a drum
With the beat, beat, beat of your heart.

The Pahu! Fa'atete!
Lali! Pati, Po!

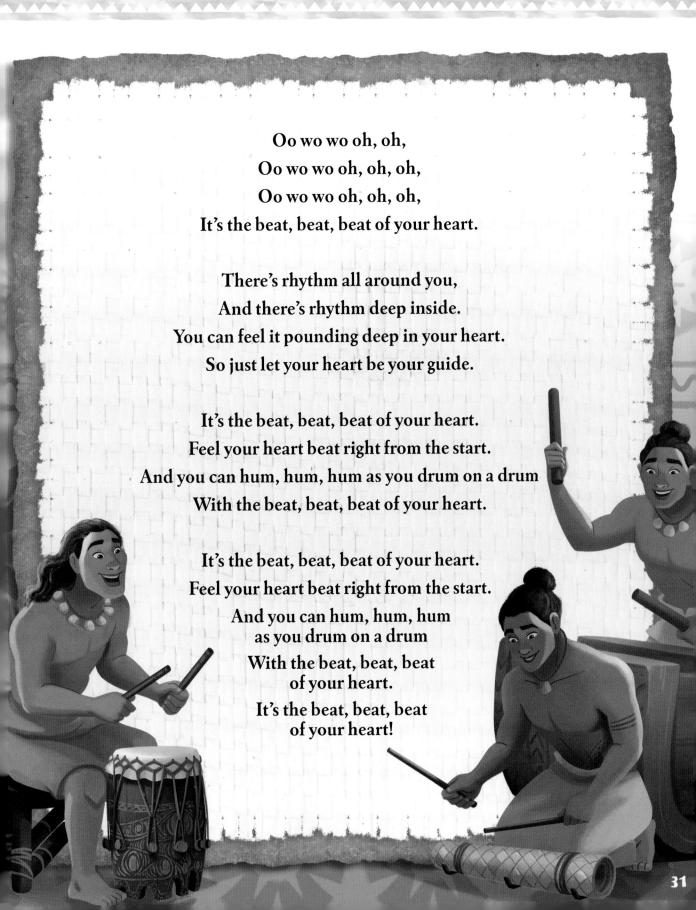

Oo wo wo oh, oh,
Oo wo wo oh, oh, oh,
Oo wo wo oh, oh, oh,
It's the beat, beat, beat of your heart.

There's rhythm all around you,
And there's rhythm deep inside.
You can feel it pounding deep in your heart.
So just let your heart be your guide.

It's the beat, beat, beat of your heart.
Feel your heart beat right from the start.
And you can hum, hum, hum as you drum on a drum
With the beat, beat, beat of your heart.

It's the beat, beat, beat of your heart.
Feel your heart beat right from the start.
And you can hum, hum, hum
as you drum on a drum
With the beat, beat, beat
of your heart.
It's the beat, beat, beat
of your heart!

MESSAGE TO PARENTS & CAREGIVERS

The steady beat is the heartbeat of music—the foundation on which we build rhythms and melodies.

Babies express a sense of steady beat through rocking, nodding, patting and kicking. Toddlers learn how to control their bodies and a steady beat helps them as they gain mobility skills, like walking and running. For preschoolers, learning a steady beat encourages the development of more precise skills like marching, bouncing balls, and learning to write and draw.

With music, young children often "feel" the beat instinctively and express it by moving their bodies. Parents and caregivers can help children discover and develop a steady beat by having them imitate simple body percussion: clapping hands, tapping thighs, and stomping feet.

Playing drums is another excellent way for young children to experience and internalize a steady beat. As children begin to "feel" the beat internally, they are able to express (play) the beat on the drum. The physical sensation of playing the drum and hearing the sound it makes allows the child to move the internalized beat from inside to outside—an exciting and rewarding experience for preschoolers.

For some children, finding a steady beat can be difficult—but the process can still be fun. Like many skills, developing a strong sense of a steady beat is best introduced at an early age. Create a daily routine that includes opportunities for steady beat play and rhythmic engagement. These activities will not only foster motor skills, but communication skills as well.

Access online content:
www.halleonard.com/exploremusic/00160410